CULTURAL CONTRIBUTIONS FROM

INDIA

DECIMALS, SHAMPOO, AND MORE

GREAT CULTURES, GREAT IDEAS

MADELINE TYLER

PowerKiDS press

Published in 2019 by The Rosen
Publishing Group, Inc.
29 East 21st Street, New York, NY 10010

Cataloging-in-Publication Data

Names: Tyler, Madeline.
Title: Cultural contributions from India: decimals, shampoo, and more / Madeline Tyler.
Description: New York : PowerKids Press, 2019. | Series: Great cultures, great ideas | Includes glossary and index.
Identifiers: LCCN ISBN 9781538338261 (pbk.) | ISBN 9781538338254 (library bound) | ISBN 9781538338278 (6 pack)
Subjects: LCSH: India--Juvenile literature. | India--Social life and customs--Juvenile literature. | India--Civilization--Juvenile literature. | Civilization--Indic influences.
Classification: LCC DS407.T954 2019 | DDC 954--dc23

Written by: Madeline Tyler
Edited by: Holly Duhig
Designed by: Gareth Liddington

Photo credits
Abbreviations: l-left, r-right, b-bottom, t-top, c-center, m-middle.

Front Cover – gresei, antalogiya, ScofieldZa, demidoff, Valentina Razumova, NYS, monticello, Hlorgeksidin, 2 - Kristin Ruhs, 4 - stocker1970, Jakkarin Apikornrat, Creative-Touch, AJP, Sirisak Chantorn, Memory Stockphoto, piyaphong, 5 - AJ Fraines, DisobeyAr, Sata Production, Jennifer Lam, Kamil Macniak, tusharkoley, 6 - Magdanatka, I am Corona, hxdyl, 7 - sebasnoo, Heath Doman, Maximumvector, charnsitr, 8 - Sapsiwai, ixpert, 9 - YURY TARANIK, 10 - AJP, NIKS ADs, piyaphong, 11 - Ami Parikh, espies, phive, 12 - Sergey Clocikov, shimbu saini, Steve Lovegrove, Bariskina, Micha Weber, 13 - Xubayr Mayo, rustycanuck, 14 - Pikoso.kz, mail11, tataphongpict, People Image Studio, 15 - Bsnigam, Lina Istomina, GlebSStock, 16 - saiko3p, Dey.sandip. 17 - Scott Biales, David Evison, Waj, 18 -Sten Rudrich, Smarta, Santhosh Varghese, 19 - Darko Manasic, Guryanov Andrey, Kalcutta, 20 - Abel Tumik, Africa Studio, Aled Erofeenkov, Jesse Davis, Madlen, Cabeca de Marmore, 21 - wong yu liang, Joe Gough, Brent Hofacker, its_al_dente, wong yu liang, 22 - dubassy, JSR, Giuseppe_R, 23 - Todd Taulman Photography, The_Pixel, dubassy, Wichai TREETHIDTAPHAT, 24 - Sergey Peterman, Monkey Business Images, Fotokvadrat, 25 - Jain Miniature, Stephen Rees, vable, 26 - BCFC, sursad, aodaodaodaod, 27 - sirtravelalot, Dmitry Kalinovsky, AlikeYou, Maridav, 28 - Hugh Llewelyn, Winning 7799, 29 - Alona_S, Darko Manasic, SK Herb, Evgeny Atamanenko, Skyprayer2005.

Images are courtesy of Shutterstock.com. With thanks to Getty Images, Thinkstock Photo and iStockphoto.

Manufactured in the United States of America

CPSIA Compliance Information: Batch #CSPK18: For Further Information contact Rosen Publishing, New York, New York at 1-800-237-9932.

CONTENTS

Page 4 What Is Culture?
Page 6 Global Culture
Page 8 Where Is India?

CULTURE, TRADITION, AND CELEBRATION

Page 10 Festivals
Page 12 Henna and Mehndi
Page 14 Yoga and Meditation
Page 16 Taj Mahal
Page 18 Bollywood
Page 20 Food

INVENTIONS AND DISCOVERIES

Page 22 Mathematics
Page 24 Games
Page 26 Cotton Clothing
Page 28 Toilets
Page 30 Shampoo
Page 31 Glossary
Page 32 Index

Words that look like this are explained in the glossary on page 31.

WHAT IS CULTURE?

If you were to travel around the world, visiting lots of countries on the way, you would probably notice that certain things around you would not be the same as they are at home. The countries and places you visit, and the people you meet, would have different languages, customs, and ways of doing things. The food might be different, the way people dress might be different, and even the laws and rules might be different to what you know at home. All of these things, when put together, make up what we call the culture of a place.

A HOUSE IN CHINA MIGHT LOOK VERY DIFFERENT THAN ONE IN THE UK!

WHAT MAKES UP A CULTURE?

Shared ideas and traditions that make up a culture can include:

- LAWS
- FOOD
- LEADERS
- SYMBOLS
- BELIEFS
- CEREMONIES
- HOLIDAYS
- FAMILIES
- SCHOOLS
- SPECIAL BUILDINGS
- HOSPITALS
- ENTERTAINMENT

A culture can also be shared by a group of people who might not live near each other, but who share a way of life. People who like the same music or hobbies can share a culture. People who all belong to the same religion can be said to share a culture, no matter where they live.

BEAUTIFUL HENNA TATTOOS ARE PART OF INDIAN CULTURE. MANY INDIAN BRIDES AROUND THE WORLD PRACTICE THIS CULTURAL TRADITION.

Our culture is a big part of our identity. Having a distinctive culture is what makes places or people unique. Knowing you belong to a particular culture is a good feeling. It's nice to share our culture with other people. If we are in a culture we recognize, we understand what to do or how to act.

DIFFERENT CULTURES GREET EACH OTHER IN DIFFERENT WAYS – A HANDSHAKE, A BOW, OR EVEN A KISS!

GLOBAL CULTURE

Even though every culture is different and unique, many cultures also have lots of things in common. We can learn a lot from other cultures, and share the things we know and like. In the past, when people started travelling to other cultures, they swapped and shared their food. They shared traditions and knowledge, and people started to adopt things from other cultures into their own. For example, British people see drinking tea as part of their cultural identity – but tea is originally from China and is also an important part of Japanese culture.

AFTERNOON TEA, WITH CAKES AND SANDWICHES, IS A TRADITIONAL PART OF ENGLISH CULTURE.

IN JAPAN, THE TEA CEREMONY IS AN IMPORTANT CULTURAL RITUAL.

TEA WAS ORIGINALLY FROM CHINA AND ORIGINATED DURING THE SHANG DYNASTY.

It is also really interesting to explore other cultures and discover new and exciting ways of doing things! We can share our ideas and learn new things when cultures meet.

MY CULTURE, YOUR CULTURE, OUR CULTURE

Adopting ideas from other cultures can lead to really interesting results. Many cultures take inspiration from others and adapt and change their traditions and customs to make them their own. Putting two ideas from two different cultures together can produce new and exciting things. Did you know that a pizza in Italy will look very different from a pizza in the US? Italians introduced pizza, a traditional Italian dish, to the Americans living in the US. A traditional Italian pizza has a thin, crispy crust, and lots of tomato, but only a small amount of mozzarella cheese. An American pizza has a thick, fluffy base, is smothered in cheese, and can have lots of different toppings – meats, fish, even pineapple! Both cultures share a love for pizza, but each culture has their own way of doing things!

TRADITIONAL ITALIAN PIZZA

WHICH PIZZA DO YOU PREFER? ITALIAN, AMERICAN, OR MAYBE A SLICE OF EACH?

AMERICAN PIZZA

WHERE IS INDIA?

India is a huge country in Asia. It is found in the Northern and Eastern **hemispheres**. India is so big that it once formed the whole of the Indian subcontinent. This is now divided between India, Pakistan, and Bangladesh.

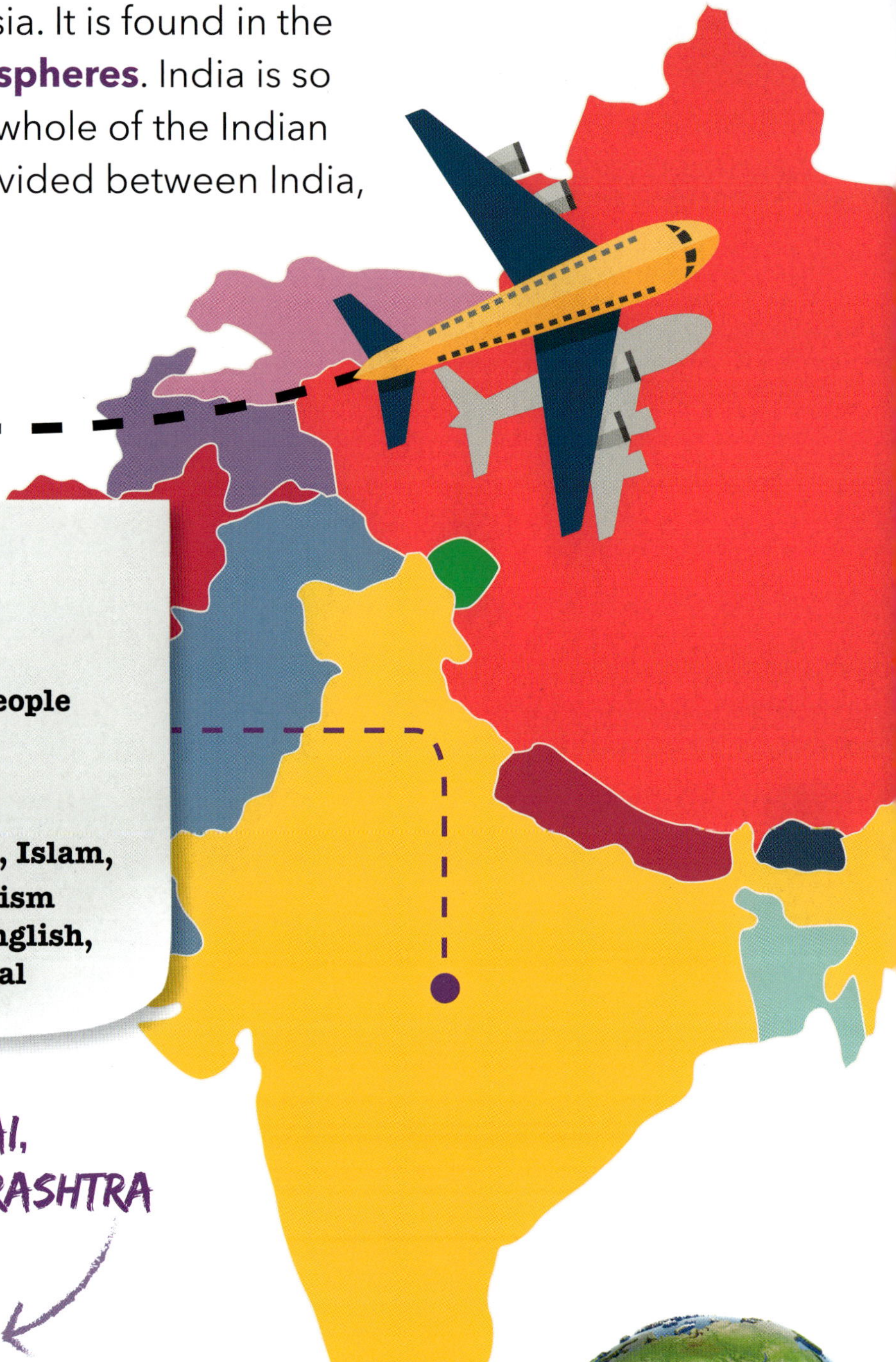

India

Capital city: New Delhi
Continent: Asia
Population: 1,300,000,000 people
Size: 1,269,000 square miles (3,286,694 sq km)
Currency: Rupee
Major religion(s): Hinduism, Islam, Christianity, Sikhism, Buddhism
Main language(s): Hindu, English, and more than 20 other official languages!

MUMBAI, MAHARASHTRA

CAN YOU SPOT INDIA?

STATES AND ZONES

India can be split into different zones: The Northern Zone, the Central Zone, the Eastern Zone, the North-Eastern Zone, the Southern Zone, and the Western Zone. These zones are made up of states, and each zone has its own council to look after it.

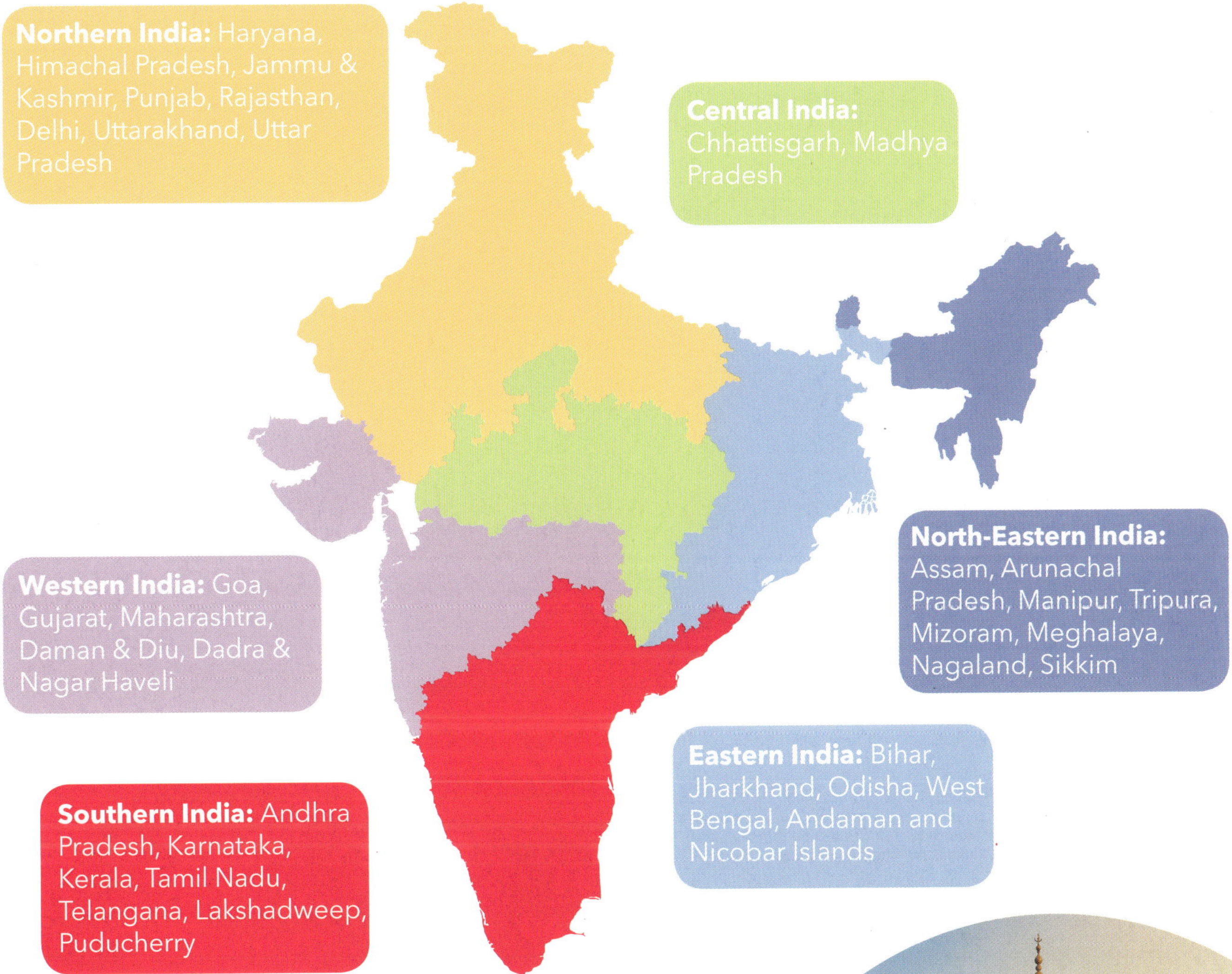

TAJ MAHAL, UTTAR PRADESH

Each region in India is different. There are many languages, religions, climates, and ways of life. This makes Indian culture very diverse.

FESTIVALS

There are many religions in India, but the largest is Hinduism. Hinduism is a collection of beliefs with no single **founder**, no single holy book, and no agreed set of teachings. This makes it very unique. Many people think of Hinduism as being the oldest living religion in the world.

THIS IS GANESH, ONE OF THE HINDU GODS.

HOLI

Holi is a Hindu festival that celebrates the arrival of spring. Bonfires are lit in the streets and people throw paint all over their friends, family, and even strangers! During Holi, everyone is equal – when people are covered in paint, it is difficult to see who they are, how old they are, or where they are from. Holi is full of dancing, laughter, music, and fun.

PEOPLE THROW COLORED POWDERS (GULAL) AT EACH OTHER.

Holi is also popular with non-Hindus around the world. Cities in Europe and the US hold their own Holi celebrations that are not religious. In the US, Holi is celebrated as the Festival of Color. Thousands of people gather to play and party together.

HINDUISM IS NOW THE FOURTH-LARGEST RELIGION IN THE WORLD!

DIWALI

Diwali is another important festival in Hinduism, but it is also celebrated by **Jains** and Sikhs. Diwali is also called the "Festival of Lights." It usually falls between the middle of October and the middle of November, but the exact date changes every year.

It celebrates light over darkness, good over evil, and knowledge over **ignorance**. People traditionally decorate the streets and their homes with oil lamps called diyas. For many Hindus, Diwali honors Lakshmi, the Hindu goddess of **wealth**. These lamps are believed to help Lakshmi find people's homes to bless them for the new year.

FIREWORKS AND SPARKLERS ARE OFTEN USED DURING DIWALI.

During Diwali, Hindus get together with their families to enjoy a big feast. People like to buy gifts for their friends and family during Diwali. Traditional gifts include sweets and dried fruits, but many Hindus now buy other things to give as presents too.

HENNA AND MEHNDI

WHAT IS HENNA?

Henna paste is a popular dye in India made from the henna plant. Henna has been used in Asia, the Middle East, and North Africa for thousands of years. It can be used to dye skin, hair, fingernails, and even fabrics like wool or leather. Henna is now most popular as a way of decorating a person's skin with beautiful and **intricate** patterns.

A HENNA PLANT

HENNA CAN ALSO BE USED TO COLOR HAIR RED, BROWN, OR BLACK.

People in India buy dried henna powder, mix it with water, and use it to paint patterns on their skin. This tradition of creating henna designs on someone's skin is called "mehndi."

Mehndi is thousands of years old and is common in both India and Hinduism. It is traditionally used for celebrations like weddings, birthdays, and holidays or festivals.

EVEN THOUGH HENNA PASTE LOOKS DARK GREEN, IT DYES THE SKIN ORANGE!

WHAT IS MEHNDI?

Mehndi is an important part of traditional Indian weddings. The night before the wedding, the bride hosts a mehndi party for her family and friends. A mehndi artist paints beautiful henna designs on the bride's hands and feet. The designs symbolize joy, beauty, and becoming **wiser**. They can take hours to complete! Indian mehndi designs are very intricate and floral. Every mehndi design is always unique because mehndi artists draw from their imagination and do not use a stencil. The night is a big celebration and is full of games and dancing.

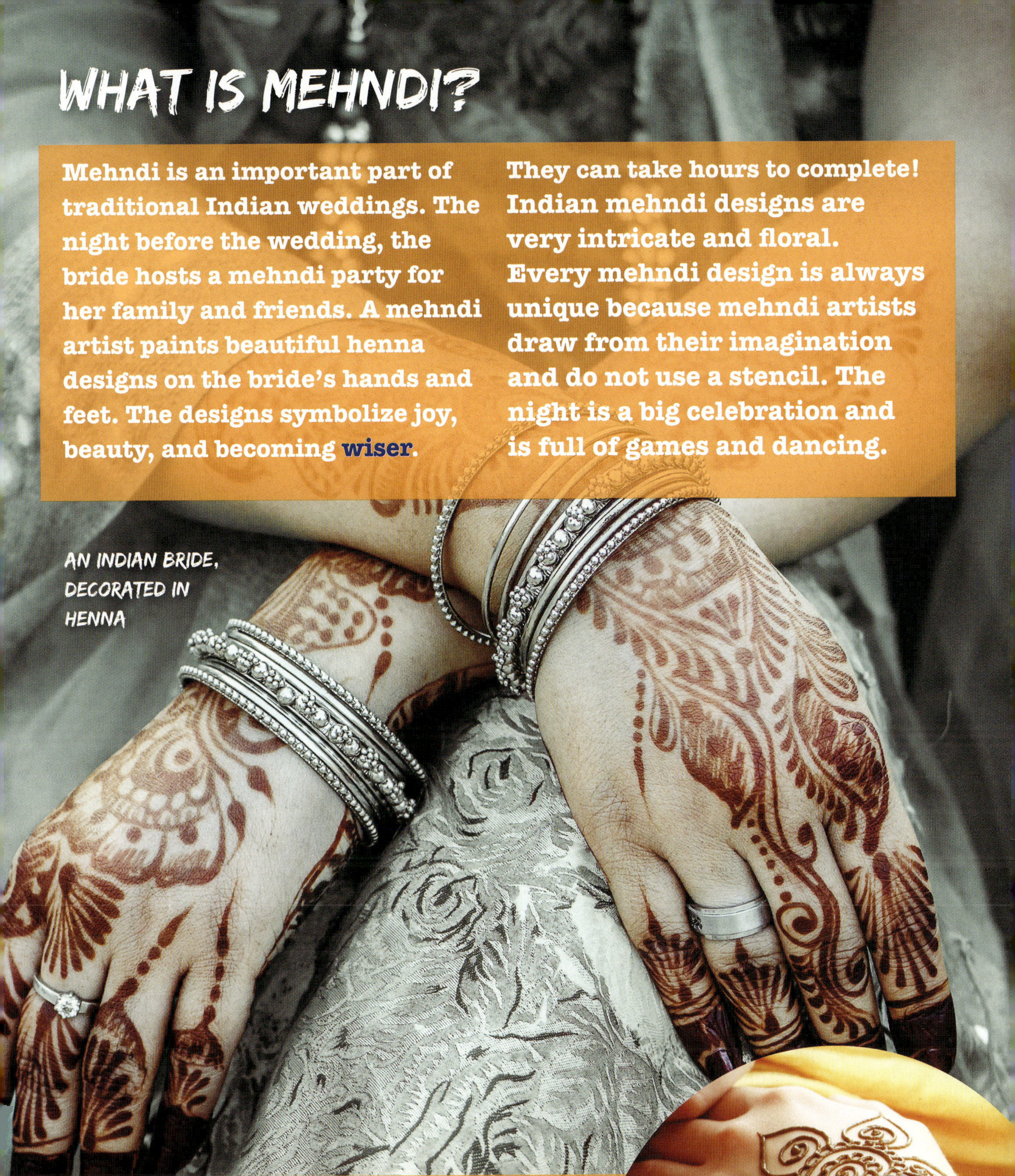

AN INDIAN BRIDE, DECORATED IN HENNA

Mehndi has become more popular around the world, especially among women and girls in Europe and the US. Mehndi artists work all over the world, creating beautiful henna designs.

YOGA AND MEDITATION

Buddhism began in India around 2,500 years ago. It is a religion focused on calmness and reflection. Personal **spiritual** development is important to a Buddhist. This means that you should never be greedy or unkind, and should always try to help people around you. An important part of Buddhism is concentrating on your own spiritual journey. This can be done through yoga and meditation.

THIS IS A STATUE OF BUDDHA, THE FOUNDER OF BUDDHISM.

MEDITATION

People have been meditating in Asia for thousands of years. Meditation is a way of emptying your mind of any thoughts, feelings, or worries. It is practiced in many religions.

Some people believe that having a clear mind allows you to be at peace with yourself and the world around you. Some forms of meditation involve concentrating on the way you breathe. Buddhism teaches you how to clear your mind and control your breathing through meditation.

MANY PEOPLE MEDITATE TO LEAD A CALMER AND HAPPIER LIFE.

MEDITATING ALLOWS THIS BUDDHIST MONK TO BECOME PEACEFUL AND FOCUSED.

YOGA

Just like meditation, yoga is an ancient practice and is important to Hinduism and Buddhism. It started in India around 5,000 years ago and is now popular all around the world. When people first started practicing yoga, it was a very spiritual act. Yoga is made up of different positions and poses. A yoga pose involves holding your body in a certain way, sometimes to make a shape. A person has to be strong and flexible to stay in the same position for such a long time.

SOME PEOPLE WHO PRACTICE YOGA BELIEVE THAT THE HINDU GOD SHIVA WAS THE FIRST YOGI. IN IMAGES, SHIVA IS USUALLY REPRESENTED AS MEDITATING OR IN THE SUKHASANA POSE.

THE ADIYOGI SHIVA STATUE, INDIA

When you practice yoga, it is important to focus on your body, your breathing, and your mind. Yoga helps you lead a healthy life and is good for physical and mental health.

TAJ MAHAL

The Taj Mahal is a beautiful Islamic **mausoleum** in the Central Zone of India. The building of the Taj Mahal was started in 1631 by Shah Jahan, an emperor who ruled over the **Mughal Empire** in the 17th century. Shah Jahan wanted to build the Taj Mahal for his wife Mumtaz Mahal, who died giving birth to their 14th child. Shah Jahan and Mumtaz Mahal are both buried in tombs inside the Taj Mahal.

IT TOOK 22,000 PEOPLE AND 1,000 ELEPHANTS TO BUILD THE TAJ MAHAL!

The Taj Mahal consists of a tomb, **mosque**, guest house, and main gate. The tomb is the most famous building and is made from white marble. Marble is a type of stone, and it was brought from all over India and Central Asia. It took 21 years to complete all the buildings that are part of the Taj Mahal.

THE TAJ MAHAL MOSQUE IS MADE OF RED SANDSTONE.

TOURISM AT THE TAJ MAHAL

The Taj Mahal is one of the Seven Wonders of the World and is also a UNESCO world heritage site. UNESCO stands for The United Nations Educational, Scientific, and Cultural Organization. This means that the building is important to Indian culture and should be protected. It is one of the most famous landmarks in India, attracting around 8 million visitors every year!

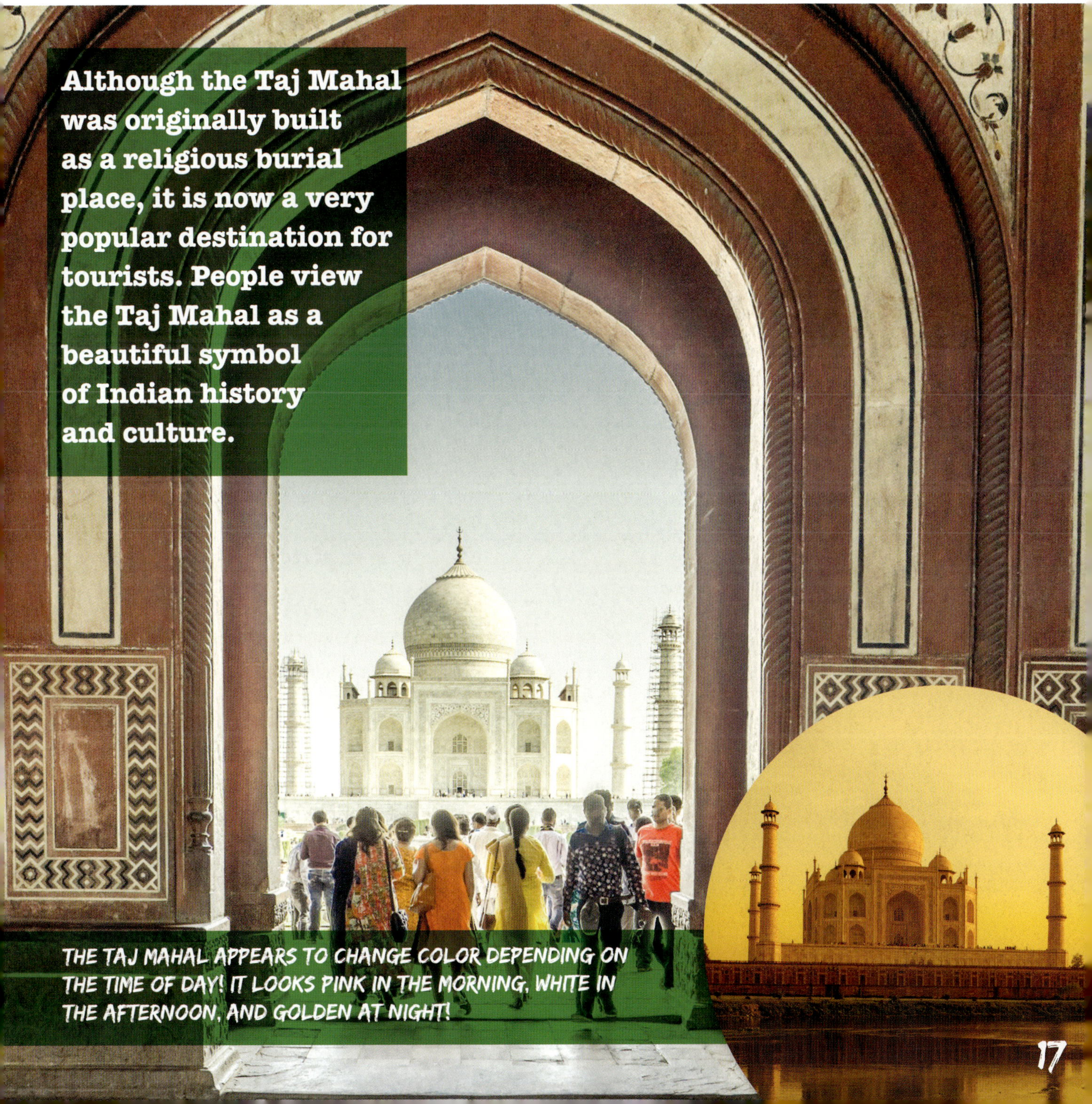

Although the Taj Mahal was originally built as a religious burial place, it is now a very popular destination for tourists. People view the Taj Mahal as a beautiful symbol of Indian history and culture.

THE TAJ MAHAL APPEARS TO CHANGE COLOR DEPENDING ON THE TIME OF DAY! IT LOOKS PINK IN THE MORNING, WHITE IN THE AFTERNOON, AND GOLDEN AT NIGHT!

BOLLYWOOD

Hollywood is a neighborhood in Los Angeles, California, famous for the films it produces and the actors and directors who live nearby. But what about Bollywood? Bollywood is like the Indian version of Hollywood.

Its name is a play on words – the B comes from Bombay, which is what Mumbai used to be called. Bollywood is based in Mumbai and is the center of the Hindi-language film **industry**.

THE HOLLYWOOD SIGN, LOS ANGELES

MUMBAI, INDIA

Bollywood films are very different to Hollywood films.

- Bollywood films are very long! Most are three hours long, sometimes even longer.
- They are very colorful. The performers wear extravagant clothing and jewelry.
- There is lots of music and dancing in many Bollywood films.
- Most Bollywood films have a happy ending.

NOT ALL FILMS FROM INDIA ARE BOLLYWOOD FILMS. TAMIL, TELUGU, AND BENGALI FILMS ARE ALSO POPULAR IN INDIA.

Bollywood began in the 1930s and is now one of the biggest film industries in India. India produces more than 1,000 films a year, and many of these are Bollywood films. This is a lot more than the US, which releases around 700 films a year. In India, 2.7 billion movie tickets are sold every year. Three Bollywood films have been nominated for "Best Foreign Language Film" at the Academy Awards (the Oscars) since 1957, but none have won yet.

THE THREE NOMINATED FILMS WERE: MOTHER INDIA, SALAAM BOMBAY!, AND LAGAAN.

CHOREOGRAPHY IS VERY IMPORTANT IN BOLLYWOOD FILMS. DANCES AND FIGHT SCENES ARE PLANNED VERY CAREFULLY SO THAT THE PERFORMERS FOLLOW THE BEST ROUTINES.

FOOD

SPICES

Have you ever eaten something that makes your mouth feel like it is on fire? This is what spicy food tastes like. Many spices, such as turmeric and saffron, come from India and are **exported** around the world. Spices are important in Indian cooking and are used in curries and other dishes.

CHILI PEPPERS ARE SPICY!

Portugal was the first country in modern history to export spices from India to Europe, in 1501. Hundreds of years before this, black pepper was exported from India to Greece as early as 400 BC. The Roman Empire was also interested in Indian spices and sent 120 ships to India every year to fetch and import black pepper. India is now home to the largest spice market in Asia! It is called Khari Baoli and can be found in Old Delhi.

SPICE MARKET

SPICES ARE NOW USED IN COOKING ALL AROUND THE WORLD.

BLACK PEPPER

DISHES

Indian **cuisine** is mostly made up of rice, spices, vegetables, and fruits. One of the most popular types of Indian dish is curry. Curries are heavily spiced and contain fish, meat, or vegetables. They are usually served with steamed rice and Indian breads, like naan bread. Some other popular Indian foods are samosas and onion bhajis. These are often eaten as a starter or as a side dish.

Some people in India do not eat certain foods because of their faith or religion. For example:

- In Hinduism, the cow is a sacred animal, so eating beef is forbidden.
- People who follow Jainism are vegetarian and cannot eat any meat.
- Muslims do not eat pork because it is written in their holy book, the Koran.

Lots of food in India is vegetarian so that it follows all these rules.

NAAN IS A FLATBREAD POPULAR IN INDIA. RAISINS AND SPICES ARE SOMETIMES ADDED TO GIVE THE BREAD MORE FLAVOR.

MATHEMATICS

DECIMAL NUMBER SYSTEM

The numbers we use are very important. They are on clocks, telephones, calendars, and on the pages of books. We use numbers every day.

From 1 to 435 to 278,973 ... No matter how high you count, you will only ever use 10 different symbols–1, 2, 3, 4, 5, 6, 7, 8, 9, and 0. These numbers, or digits, are called Hindu-Arabic numerals. They were first created in India in the 6th or 7th century AD.

THE NUMBERS WE USE TODAY CAME FROM EARLY HINDU-ARABIC NUMBERS.

The Hindu-Arabic numerals are grouped by tens. This is called a decimal number system. Ten ones are represented by 10, ten tens are represented by 100, and ten hundreds are represented by 1,000.

Thousand	Hundred	Ten	One
4	7	3	1

=4,731

WE HAVE TEN DIGITS ON OUR HANDS, JUST LIKE THE TEN DIGITS OF THE DECIMAL NUMBER SYSTEM.

ZERO

Zero is one of the Hindu-Arabic numerals. India was the first country to introduce zero to the world. Many people believe that the Indian man Brahmagupta was the first person to use zero as a number. The early symbol for zero was a dot on the page, not the 0 that we know today. The invention of zero allows us to tell the difference between 10, 100, and 1,000.

RULERS

Do you use a ruler at school for measuring things? Rulers are very useful for measuring how long, tall, or wide something is. People in the Indus Valley were using rulers over 3,000 years ago to measure the size of bricks. All bricks in the Indus Valley were the same size – the length, depth, and height were in the ratio of 4:2:1. The height was half of the depth, and the depth was half of the length. This shows how accurate their rulers were!

GAMES

CHESS

Chess is very popular and is one of the oldest board games in the world. It can be quite a difficult game to learn, but over 600 million people now play it regularly. The International Olympic Committee have now recognized it as a sport, but it is not played at the Olympics yet!

Chess was invented in India around 1,400 years ago. The original chess game was quite similar to the one we know now. It was called "chaturanga." Both chaturanga and chess have pieces with different moves, and winning the game depends on the "king" piece.

Chess was eventually carried to the Middle East, East Asia, North Africa and Europe in the 11th century. The rules and pieces have changed a lot since then, but without chaturanga there would be no such thing as chess.

IF A PLAYER CAPTURES THE OPPONENT'S KING, THEY WIN THE GAME!

VIKINGS BROUGHT CHESS TO ICELAND AND ENGLAND AROUND 1,000 YEARS AGO!

SNAKES AND LADDERS

The game of Snakes and Ladders was invented by Hindu spiritual teachers in India, and was originally called "Moksha Patamu." Moksha Patamu taught players about karma.

A snake would send a person down to a picture of demons, while a ladder would allow a person to climb up to an image of a Hindu god. These different outcomes showed a young child the effects of good deeds and bad deeds.

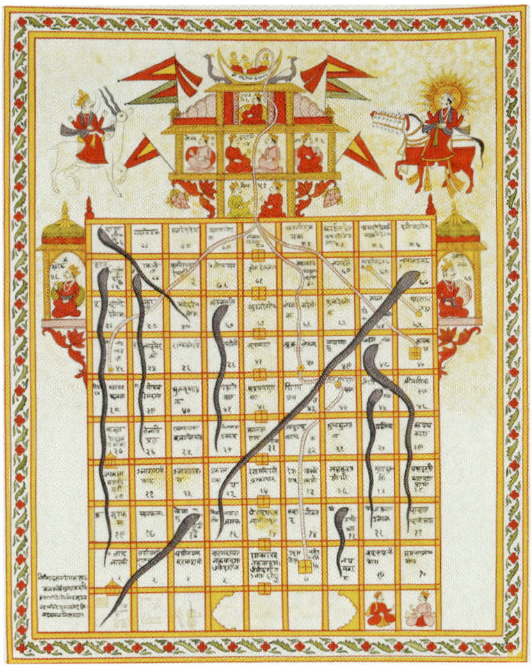

THIS IS A JAIN VERSION OF SNAKES AND LADDERS FROM THE 19TH CENTURY CALLED "JNANA BAZI."

SNAKES AND LADDERS GAMES CAN SOMETIMES BE FOUND IN CHILDREN'S PLAYGROUNDS.

When Moksha Patamu came to Britain in the 19th century, it was renamed Snakes and Ladders. Many of the Hindu parts of the game were removed. Modern versions of Snakes and Ladders are not usually religious or focused on moral lessons. Now Hindus and non-Hindus all over the world play this game for fun.

COTTON CLOTHING

What material is your T-shirt made from? If you look at the label, you will see that it probably has cotton in it. Cotton is a very useful plant that is used to make clothes. It can also be used to make bed \sheets, towels, and, of course, cotton balls. Cotton is used all over the world today. Who made products from cotton first?

COTTON PLANT

THIS WOMAN IS COLLECTING COTTON FROM A FIELD.

The Indus Valley was one of the first areas to begin **cultivating** cotton thousands of years ago. Hundreds of years later, the Mughal Empire, and later India, started exporting lots of products and materials across Asia and Europe. One of the most important products made in India at this time was cotton material. By the 18th century, Indian cotton had become so popular that it was being exported to Japan, the US, and South America.

PEOPLE HAVE BEEN USING COTTON FOR MANY YEARS. IN FACT, PEOPLE IN INDIA HAVE BEEN MAKING COTTON FABRICS FOR 6,000 YEARS!

India was the first place where cotton was grown to make clothes and, for many years after, cotton was only grown in India, Mexico, and Peru. Indian cotton was very expensive for people in Europe and was treated like a luxury because it had to be carried very long distances. Around 1,200 years ago, Arab merchants carried cotton to Europe and it became more affordable for people to buy.

THIS WOMAN IS MAKING CLOTH.

Cotton materials and products are now made in large factories all over the world. Using machines allows more cloth to be made in a faster time – this makes it cheaper. Cotton is now quite a cheap material and most clothes have some cotton in them.

COTTON CAN BE DYED LOTS OF DIFFERENT COLORS.

TOILETS

WHAT DID ONE TOILET SAY TO THE OTHER? YOU LOOK FLUSHED!

Can you imagine if toilets did not flush? They would be very nasty and very smelly. Although the flushing toilet was invented in 1596, it did not become a common feature in people's homes until around 300 years later. This early toilet is quite different to ones we are used to today. It had a flush chain instead of a handle.

PEOPLE WOULD FLUSH THE TOILET BY PULLING THE CHAIN.

THIS IS WHAT MANY MODERN TOILETS LOOK LIKE.

They had no handle or chain, but toilets in the Indus Valley were some of the first ones that used water as a flushing system. This kept towns in the Indus Valley clean and **sanitary**.

HERE ARE SOME WAYS TO SAY 'TOILET' IN OTHER LANGUAGES!

Banheiro
Musqusha
Halepaku
トイレ
TOALETT NECESEJO

Toilets in the Indus Valley were very innovative.

1. **People flushed the toilets by pouring jars of water into the toilet bowl. (This might sound old-fashioned, but at the time it was genius!)**
2. **The toilet waste was carried away by the water through clay pipes.**
3. **The clay pipes led to a drain in the street.**
4. **The waste eventually ended up in soak pits.**
5. **It was someone's job to dig the soak pits and take the waste away.**
6. **Toilets were kept clean and the streets were waste-free!**

THESE SIGNS ARE USUALLY USED FOR RESTROOMS.

FLUSHING FACTS!

- **The average person will spend three years of their life sitting on the toilet!**
- **World Toilet Day is on November 19th.**
- **The average toilet gets flushed eight times a day.**
- **Most people visit the toilet 2,500 times a year!**
- **Flushing the toilet uses round 6-12 liters of water!**

SHAMPOO

"Shampoo" is a funny word. It comes from the Hindi word "champo." "Champo" means "to press," like giving someone a **massage**, or when you rub your head to wash your hair!

This is no coincidence – early forms of shampoo were being used in India hundreds of years ago and were used like a massage.

Sapindus fruits were boiled with dried herbs and then massaged onto a person's body and **scalp**. This is champo! People from Europe saw how soft and shiny champo left a person's hair and took the idea back home. They renamed the product "shampoo." It was very expensive and only very **wealthy** people could afford it. Shampoo has changed a lot since then. Liquid shampoo comes in bottles of different shapes, sizes, and colors.

THE FRUIT OF SAPINDUS ARE SOMETIMES CALLED SOAPBERRIES OR SOAPNUTS. THEY CREATE A LATHER AND HAVE BEEN USED AS A TYPE OF SOAP FOR HUNDREDS OF YEARS.

SOAPBERRIES OR SOAPNUTS

GLOSSARY

choreography	arranging dances and planning out dance moves
cuisine	a type or style of cooking
cultivating	growing and caring for a plant or crop
exported	sent to another country for sale
founder	the person that starts or establishes something, like a religion
hemispheres	sections of the Earth, either Northern, Southern, Eastern, or Western
ignorance	lack of knowledge or awareness
industry	businesses that specialize in something specific, e.g. the film industry
Indus Valley	an area in India and Pakistan near to the Indus River, home to the ancient Indus Valley civilization
innovative	to do something in a new way that has not been done before
intricate	very detailed
Jains	followers of Jainism, a religion in India
karma	the idea that a person's actions decide their future, e.g. good actions will lead to a good future
lather	the foam that is made by mixing soap with water
massage	rubbing and pressing the body to help blood circulation and relax muscles
mausoleum	a large building that holds a tomb inside
mosque	a religious place where Muslims worship
Mughal Empire	a group that ruled much of India and Pakistan in the 16th and 17th centuries
ratio	the relationship between two things based on the amount or measure of something
sanitary	clean and not dangerous to health
scalp	the skin on top of the head, covered with hair
Sikhism	a religion in India that follows one god
spiritual	related to religion or spirits, rather than the physical world
wealth	a large amount of something, e.g. money or possessions
wealthy	having lots of money
wiser	having a better understanding and judgment of what is good or true

INDEX

B

Buddhism 8, 14-15

C

California 18
chess 24
cotton 26-27
curry 20-21

D

decimal 22
Diwali 11

E

export 20, 26

F

festivals 10-12
films 18-19

G

Ganesh 10

H

henna 5, 12-13
Hinduism 8, 10-12, 15, 21, 25
Holi 10
Hollywood 18

I

Indus Valley 23, 26, 28, 29
Islam 8, 16

J

Jainism 11, 21, 25

K

karma 25

L

Lakshmi 11

M

Mumbai 8, 18

R

religion 5, 8-10, 14-15, 17, 21, 25

S

Shah Jahan 16
Shiva 15
Sikhism 8, 11
spices 20-21

T

toilets 28-29

U

UNESCO 17

V

Vikings 24

W

wedding 12-13

Z

zero 23